REDNECK
H A I K U

Double-Wide Edition

M A R Y   K .   W I T T E

Bubba-Sized with More than 150 New Haiku!

SANTA
MONICA
PRESS

Published by:
Santa Monica Press LLC
P.O. Box 1076
Santa Monica, CA 90406-1076
1-800-784-9553
www.santamonicapress.com
books@santamonicapress.com

Printed in the United States

Santa Monica Press books are available at special quantity discounts when purchased in bulk by corporations, organizations, or groups. Please call our Special Sales department at 1-800-784-9553.

ISBN 1-59580-007-7

Library of Congress Cataloging-in-Publication Data

Witte, Mary K., 1949–
  Redneck haiku / by Mary K. Witte.— Double-wide ed.
    p. cm.
  ISBN 1-59580-007-7
  1. Rednecks—Poetry. 2. Haiku, American. I. Title.
  PS3623.I88R43 2005
  811'.6—dc22

                                        2005009683

Cover and interior design by Ann Buckley
Production by Lynda "Cooldog" Jakovich

Mom, thanks for everything, especially the neat genes.

Haiku: three line verse,
  five, seven, five syllables,
  captures a moment.

Redneck: person who
  lacks class but enjoys a life
  without rich folks' rules.

Double-Wide: two part
  mobile home makes mansion for
  redneck nouveau riche.

Willie curses thief

who steals chain saw from him that

he stole from Bubba.

Orthodontist buys

new bass boat after seeing

Bobby McGill's teeth.

Wedding night fireworks

as Flo's ex-husband threatens

to bring back the kids.

Bug zapper becomes

Roy's entertainment after

TV repossessed.

Redemption has helped

Uncle Walter's way of life.

Old beer cans, not church.

Go to the dentist?

Grandpa went once, and now look.

He has no teeth left.

Short cut to Memphis

discovered by Uncle Zeke

takes four times as long.

Turkey fryer bought

from cable shopping channel

burns down trailer park.

Jake eats standing up

with butt full of buckshot from

watermelon theft.

Betty Lou surprised

to learn you *can* get pregnant

in church parking lot.

Clyde's job prospects end
after his appearance on
"Criminals at Large."

Goat was barbecued

after eating seat covers

in Bubba's new truck.

Long-haired, foxy girl,

   has perfect look except for

   two missing front teeth.

Bobby learns to read,

sets a family record.

He's only thirteen.

Todd sports full arm cast
following leap from barn loft
on double-dawg dare.

Stored in shirt pocket

old match stick cleans Jake's ears, comb,

fingernails and teeth.

Bubba gets ribbing
from the guys when he is caught
crying at chick flick.

High school football game.

Clyde thrown out for bootleg beer

and harassing ref.

Belly dancing class
   keeps Flo in shape, disgraces
      her mother-in-law.

Wanda tries bowling

but quits after it costs her

two acrylic nails.

Reno is scene of

grandparents' recent wedding.

"About time," kids say.

Jake's best cowboy hat
and boots look great when worn with
wedding tuxedo.

Mixed emotions date:

Box seat NASCAR race tickets

with world's biggest geek.

Wanda returns to

Laundromat after six-pack.

Where are all her clothes?

Trade school diploma

earned by mail qualifies Dot

for plumber's helper.

Jake's Grand Canyon trip

leaves him embarrassed and sore

after mule rescue.

Hot day at Wal-Mart.

Three horse merry-go-round calls

to whining children.

Game warden stops by

to see one tagged, legal deer.

The rest are hidden.

Stopped on Vegas Strip.

    Flat tire with no spare, no jack.

        Bad luck continues.

Election crisis:

Vote for union Democrat

or black sheep cousin?

Clyde's Kodak moment:

   when pranksters tip port-a-john

   with his wife inside.

Bubba's double-wide

was a tornado target,

now an Allstate claim.

Bobby's roadside stand

sells sweet cider to tourists.

Locals get hard stuff.

At school talent show,

catching flies with his bare hands

makes Scooter a star.

Sign "Will work for food"

gets attention at roadside.

"Howdy, Uncle Clyde!"

Bubba's lost weekend

leaves him broke, hung over and

trying to make bail.

Seven months pregnant
at first marriage, Flo boldly
wears white wedding dress.

High school football team
headed for championship
'til deer season starts.

Redneck Olympics

start when Bubba wins a keg

at Cow Chip Throwing.

Lake patrol fines Jake

for out of season fishing,

beer and dynamite.

Jake and kids move to
barn loft when Wanda's snoring
drives them from the house.

When Flo goes to Mom's,
Bubba dines on canned chili,
Pepsi and Pop Tarts.

Last Las Vegas trip

spoiled by Granny's indecent

exposure arrest.

Midnight cow tipping

was favorite sport until

the sheriff showed up.

Snappy wrist action

makes Bubba the champion

of Roadkill Frisbee.

RV at Wal-Mart:

Shopping while just passing through

or putting down roots?

Roy sweating buckets.
Is it the tight wedding tux
or her dad's shotgun?

After bean dinner

Jake's bathtub looks and sounds like

a real Jacuzzi.

Clyde's Vegas winnings

barely cover truck repairs

and beer for trip home.

Fireworks wake Grandpa.

Nap disturbed, he shouts curses.

Children laugh and run.

Terror alert raised

   when Bubba's home-made fireworks

   hit county courthouse.

Wanda's new wind chime

made of kitchen utensils

she seldom uses.

Bubba's mom's cookies

    buy him perks during his stay

        at the county jail.

Jake resents spending
more on wife's steel toed shoes than
on his cowboy boots.

Heavenly Father,

keep our driver off the wall

in this NASCAR race.

Garth Brooks look-alike

causes uproar when spotted

at local cafe.

First spring barbeque:

Clyde thaws last winter's road kill

from Rosie's deep-freeze.

Engine overheats

as Jake flees highway patrol.

Chug beers or toss them?

Bubba's rear bumper,

   trailer and boat can be found

   at bottom of lake.

Favorite "cousins"

at all weddings, births and deaths:

Jim Beam, Jack Daniels.

Jake thinks downsized means
when clothes fit after he stops
drinking so much beer.

Impromptu wedding

stops before vows when bride starts

premature labor.

Bobby practices

to be perfect at new job:

"Y'all want fries 'ith that?"

Local bail bondsmen

   no longer accept phone calls

      from Bubba or Jake.

When Pam is pregnant
local stores can't keep stocks of
sardines and ice cream.

Clyde went with cousins

   to shoot golf for the first time.

   Took his best shotgun.

Spring: Grandpa trades his
winter weight corduroy cap
for summer straw hat.

Jake backs up traffic
on busy highway driving
tractor to cornfield.

Brand new garage holds

tools, lawn mower and pickup

while porch falls off house.

Bubba's name is sewed
on his uniform shirt and
hand-tooled on his belt.

Screams at movie house

as Blaine and Jill are thrown out

for lewd behavior.

Wanda seeks culture,

buys tickets to opera.

Jake's snoring stops show.

Spring walk in the woods,
daydreaming and chewing sticks.
Oops. Poison ivy.

Interstate rest stop.

Lunchmeat sandwiches, fried pies,

ice cold grape Nehi.

Blaine's landscape job ends

when sheriff finds cannabis

in his clients' yards.

On half his paydays
Jake signs his check over to
Ed's Feed Store and Bar.

Dexter's big problem:

    wife, daughter and dog pregnant.

    All fathers unknown.

Kids toss cherry bombs.

Boat sinks, beer lost, children laugh

'til Pop swims ashore.

Clyde says hi to girls

by hitting pickup door and

howling like a dog.

Bubba rents backhoe

to dig for buried treasure.

Town phone service cut.

Grandpa's new dentures

make him lose Watermelon

Seed Spitting Contest.

Same old silly jokes

each year on April Fool's Day

but Granny still laughs.

Bobby's spring break trip

    costs him five hundred dollars

    and clinic visit.

Drunk judges award

first place in science fair to

Junior's whiskey still.

Flo is well known for
getting bleeped on her calls to
radio talk shows.

Moonshine connoisseur,

Bubba can name the maker

after just a sip.

During bad snowstorm

　newborn calf spends its first night

　　safe in Pam's kitchen.

DVD player

in tractor cab blamed for Jake's

crooked cotton rows.

Tribal casino
    lures Flo with "gifts" that cost her
    a month's salary.

Offended neighbor

tries to have Bubba jailed for

front yard deer skinning.

Sue's arm in sling when

birthday Bingo binge leaves her

with "Bingo Elbow."

Jake's state fair entry,
barbeque flavored ice cream,
awarded last place.

Even strong perfume

lavishly applied can't fight

Jane's barnyard odor.

Bubba sulks for weeks.

Click and Clack's advice to Flo

gets her truck running.

Sign on gate to Sam's
    chicken farm: "Egg Sucking Dogs
    Will be Shot on Sight."

Uncle Walter's cats

thrive on diet of mice and

neighbor's baby chicks.

Romantic weekend

  ends at motel arrival.

    Jake reserved wrong date.

Clyde's barbecue sauce

wins prize at county fair but

was bought at Safeway.

Gramps has arthritis

and now must use both hands to

unhook girlfriend's bra.

No wedding complete
without cold beer and Elvis
impersonator.

Garbage truck driver

gets confused on Bubba's street.

What stays and what goes?

New local law bans

outdoor cooking fires, prompting

move to next county.

Jake hunts and fishes
while Wanda drives forklift at
local lumber yard.

Flowers in Sue's hair

    attract wasps and bees, causing

    panic at picnic.

Drunk last Saturday

Bubba spends next four weekends

on roadside trash crew.

Clyde depressed, drinking.
Divorce cost alimony
and NASCAR tickets.

Shrimp and Buffett tunes.

Will this beer last, or do we

need a run to town?

Flo shops for new clothes

after kittens are born in

her laundry basket.

Screams disrupt state fair.

Kiddy Ferris Wheel breaks down.

Bubba stuck at top.

Old empty beer cans
found on road and sold for cash
finance keg party.

Neighbors offended

when Jake's cousins use his yard

as an RV park.

Dairy sound system
increases milk output when
Clyde plays Hank Williams.

Hitchhiking attempt
gets Bubba arrested at
Indy 500.

License plate frame on
Pam's car reads, "Cowboy crazy
and honky-tonk wild."

Teenage lovers trapped
by early winter blizzard.
Hasty wedding planned.

Beyond cell phone range,

squirrels chew wires in RV,

leaving Jake stranded.

Wal-Mart greeter weds

snack bar attendant's mother

in Garden Center.

Turquoise ring Jake bought

at highway truck stop is now

Wanda's wedding band.

School hot lunch program

shut down after cooks are caught

brewing white lightning.

Marriage proposal
was spurned but still appears on
town's water tower.

Sitting in duck blind,

    Jake listens to farm report

       between shotgun blasts.

Cowboy on the ground.

Flash of color over horns.

Thanks, rodeo clown.

Patsy's new husband
upset to find her name on
local bathroom walls.

Clyde's retirement plan:
Twenty-five dollars worth of
lottery tickets.

Sheriff won't believe

Bubba's back yard moonshine still

is just a sculpture.

State map has red stars

for all of the outlet malls

where Wanda has shopped.

Jake's free drinks and food
paid for tonight by Wanda's
slot machine losses.

Granny embroiders

beer and tobacco logos

on Bubba's best shirt.

Early spring morning.

Easter Bunny hops in sights.

Tastes great with dumplings.

Flea market sales boom
as Skeet sells items back to
folks he stole them from.

To Flo and her friends,
remodeling means buying
new Con-Tact paper.

Jake wears hip waders

to protect him from snakes on

midnight outhouse trips.

Bobby Lee's new shirt,

    bright orange, real chick magnet,

    reads "Wal-Mart Cart Crew."

Pam has ambition,

applies for clerking job at

local liquor store.

Jake tells children that

   global warming is caused by

      Wanda's hot flashes.

Bigger house? No, girl.

With this trailer and that barn,

we got lots of room.

Wanda's trip to bar

   to break up fight, drag Jake home,

    is neighborhood news.

Gert cleans teeth daily
with guests' toothbrushes at the
motel where she works.

Unemployment claim:

"Suspended driver's license

keeps me from working."

Clyde's Bait Shop beer sales
provide his tow truck business
a steady income.

Flo on winning streak,
    played slots all day and all night,
    fainted from hunger.

Wanda and Jake get
bargains on Christmas gifts at
Guns 'n' Gold Pawn Shop.

Patsy's new baby,

hidden by her weight problem,

bears nickname "Surprise."

Bubba's bowling team

holds record for beer consumed

and gutter balls thrown.

Jake winterizes

    his pickup with bag of sand,

      hay bale and shovel.

Big Vegas hotel.

Bell captain sneers at luggage:

plastic Wal-Mart bags.

Pickup, shiny red

    in Grandpa's dim memory,

        now rusts in tall weeds.

Granny's house settles.

Back door sticks shut. Front door used

first time in ten years.

After child support
Walter can either pay rent
or make truck payment.

Jake's tall tale winner
is a true recounting of
his last fishing trip.

Pam in county jail

for assaulting coach at son's

Little League ball game.

Disneyland visit

goes bad when Bubba tries to

climb the Matterhorn.

Jake's remodel lasts

fourteen years but house is still

a fixer-upper.

Bow-hunting season.

Bubba unprepared 'til he

returns to pawn shop.

Blaine quits janitor
   training program, elopes with
   beauty school dropout.

Grandpa made to sleep
on porch after going back
for seconds on beans.

Trouble starts when Flo

   buys her own remote control

   for Bubba's TV.

Sparks at work during

performance review gone bad.

Jake spends night in jail.

Chopping enough wood

    to keep house warm in winter

      keeps Granny busy.

Clyde's new monster truck
is highway patrol magnet,
also attracts chicks.

Broken toys in yard.

Traveling Bible salesman

knows he'll get this sale.

Putting fishhook in

    chef's masterpiece gets Jake tossed

    from new sushi bar.

Cat population
declines after Bobby Lee
gets birthday shotgun.

Fresh out of propane,

Bubba taps landfill methane.

Steaks taste recycled.

Scared by tornadoes,

Sue moves to California.

Earthquake hits next day.

Grandpa gets sent home
after caught taking a leak
from back of cruise ship.

At tent revival,

Betty sings "Amazing Grace."

Eighteen hear the call.

Wanda's third wedding

started an hour late to let

best man make beer run.

Plate filled to the max

at all-you-can-eat buffet.

Jake grins: "Life is good."

Bubba celebrates

Labor Day though he hasn't

worked a day all year.

Patsy's wedding dress

was bought at her ex-boyfriend's

Stepmother's yard sale.

Custody battle
  drags through court for months over
  truck and hunting dogs.

Pam blames pregnancy
on falling asleep before
boyfriend comes to bed.

All Bubba's brothers

chipped in for wide screen TV

for NASCAR season.

Landscape maintenance

is when Jake moves his best goats

into the front yard.

Aggie saves best knife

    for skinning hogs and scratching

        Lottery tickets.

Thanksgiving turkey

was deep-fried in peanut oil

As Seen On TV.

Granny told to leave

casino after remarks

offend "stud" players.

Jake's Botox treatment

   tightens up his drooping lip

    caused by dipping snuff.

Weekend barbeque

when Bubba buys side of beef

at 4-H auction.

Home Depot visit

   leads to fight when Jake wants cheap,

    but Wanda wants style.

Well-dressed trailer trash
will have muumuus and flip-flops
in matching colors.

Jim Beam under tree

is gone before Christmas toys

are all assembled.

Rest stop closure sign

panics Wanda on Route One

after large coffee.

Bubba's monster truck

   too large to fit in garage

      or fast food drive thru.

Jake's monthly bar tab
is normally more than the
payment on his truck.

Clyde's voice mail greeting:
"If the baby's really mine,
name it after me."

Bobby's yellow wake

during race gets him thrown off

high school swimming team.

How to celebrate

twenty-five years of marriage?

New hunting rifles.

Clifford nearly starves

    when pranksters hide his food stamps

    under his work boots.

Ice cold beer goes great
with illegally caught trout
fried with hushpuppies.

Bubba's front yard has
large new Nativity scene.
Church looks oddly bare.

Downtown Las Vegas.

   Gramps has no luck with hookers

    'til he takes a bath.

Jake rode to work with
wet tee-shirt contest winner
'til his wife found out.

Wanda's hip slit skirt

allows her to climb into

monster pickup truck.

Communion wine blamed

for Dale's drunk driving arrest

late on Sunday night.

July Fourth fireworks

    get hunting dogs stirred up while

      house dog whines in fear.

Empty trailer park

indicates good turnout at

Pete's clan reunion.

New Year's Day routine:

TV plays bowl games on Mute

as hangovers rule.

Mother's Day presents:

perfume and candy for Flo,

moonshine for Granny.

Bubba asked to leave

anger management class for

breaking teacher's nose.

Laid off, Jake is forced

to learn new job skills and now

stocks shelves at Wal-Mart.

Family black sheep
recently evicted from
condemned trailer park.

Flo and friends panic

when their manicurist takes

four-week vacation.

210

Cookbook collection

looks great on shelves, but Wanda

is carryout queen.

Father's Day neck tie

replaces missing tent rope

on last camping trip.

Jake's pickup declared

environmental hazard;

burns more oil than gas.

Clyde nears his deadline

on community service

before next court date.

Blue ribbon withdrawn

when "Made in China" tag found

on Jane's 4-H quilt.

Flo sets fashion at
trailer park with bouffant hair
and acrylic nails.

On his first plane ride

Bubba has panic attack

cured by a quick beer.

Freight train passing by

or tornado overhead?

Nope, Granny snoring.

Grandpa's "attorney,"

the only one he trusts, is

two-barreled shotgun.

Family plot full

so Great Uncle Delmar gets

back yard cremation.

Jake's chicken gumbo

looks like muddy swamp water,

was judged best in state.

Grandpa's new young wife
allows moonshine, draws line at
chewing tobacco.

After heavy rain,

   road sign to Bubba's place reads,

      "Road closed — boat required."

Wanda and Flo spend
most Saturday nights playing
Bingo at Elks Lodge.

Driving his RV

   in San Francisco gives Jake

      a thrill a minute.

Clyde's birthday present

is a hand-woven blanket

for favorite horse.

Trick or Treaters scared

   by Granny, without make-up,

      passed out on front porch.

Clothes dryer broken.

Clean underwear spins dry from

blades of ceiling fan.

News photo of Sam's
rescue from canal leads to
arrest for old crimes.

Family watches

for flying objects when Pam

fails to take her meds.

For Valentine's Day,

Bubba gives Flo a box of

deep-fried chicken hearts.

Family in awe:

reunion attended by

high school graduate.

Grandpa feared teeth lost

until dog pulled them from Flo's

backyard compost heap.

Uncles come to blows

during discussions whether

Earth is round or flat.

No lovin' tonight.

Jake's team in extra innings.

Wanda falls asleep.

Yosemite trip:

Shoot, cook and eat local deer.

Thousand dollar fine.

Bubba has black eye.

Neighbors say it was caused by

PMS moment.

Waving antenna

on truck cab is last trace of

stolen stereo.

Pulsing lights, low hum,

    Granny prays, hunting dogs whine:

    Spaceship lands in swamp.

Juvenile Hall stay

improves skills Homer needs for

Long-term career goals.

Jake gets pneumonia
    shirtless, drunk at football game
    played during snowstorm.

Polly likes her man

in John Deere baseball cap and

very little else.

Fried chicken, biscuits,
mashed potatoes with gravy.
Perfect summer meal.

Pam, newly pregnant,

doesn't know which guy to pick

for shotgun wedding.

Al's deal on cheap land
looks like less of a bargain
without water rights.

Rooster crows before

Mom's morning coffee and now

simmers on the stove.

Love is in the air.

Shotgun and wedding dress sales

increase every June.

Bubba got divorced,

but children from the marriage

are still his nephews.

Moonshine, shotgun shells,

Wild Turkey and motor oil.

Christmas shopping done.

High school career day.

Jake's kids cheer when he arrives

in his garbage truck.

Flo files complaint at
airport for guard's misuse of
metal sensing wand.

Washington's birthday

celebrated with moonshine.

Truck hits cherry tree.

Bubba claims to have

Dunlap's Disease, where stomach

done lapped over belt.

Last Bigfoot sighting

was just Jake taking out trash

in his underwear.

Books Available
from Santa Monica Press

American Hydrant
by Sean Crane
176 pages $24.95

**Atomic Wedgies, Wet Willies
and Other Acts of Roguery**
by Greg Tananbaum and
Dan Martin
128 pages $11.95

The Bad Driver's Handbook
by Zack Arnstein and
Larry Arnstein
192 pages $12.95

The Book of Good Habits
by Dirk Mathison
224 pages $9.95

The Butt Hello
*and other ways my cats
drive me crazy*
by Ted Meyer
96 pages $9.95

Calculated Risk
*The Extraordinary Life of
Jimmy Doolittle*
by Jonna Doolittle Hoppes
360 pages $24.95

Can a Dead Man Strike Out?
Mark S. Halfon
168 pages $11.95

The Dog Ate My Resumé
by Zack Arnstein and
Larry Arnstein
192 pages $11.95

Elvis Presley Passed Here
by Chris Epting
336 pages $16.95

**Exotic Travel Destinations
for Families**
by Jennifer M. Nichols
and Bill Nichols
360 pages $16.95

**Free Stuff & Good Deals for
Folks over 50, 2nd Ed.**
by Linda Bowman
240 pages $12.95

French for Le Snob
by Yvette Reche
400 pages $16.95

**How to Find Your Family
Roots and Write Your
Family History**
by William Latham and
Cindy Higgins
288 pages $14.95

**How to Win Lotteries,
Sweepstakes, and Contests
in the 21st Century, 2nd
Edition**
by Steve "America's
Sweepstakes King" Ledoux
224 pages $14.95

James Dean Died Here
*The Locations of America's Pop
Culture Landmarks*
by Chris Epting
312 pages $16.95

**The Largest U.S. Cities
Named after a Food**
by Brandt Maxwell
360 pages $16.95

Letter Writing Made Easy!
*Featuring Sample Letters for
Hundreds of Common Occasions*
by Margaret McCarthy
224 pages $12.95

**Letter Writing Made Easy!
Volume 2**
by Margaret McCarthy
224 pages $12.95

Life is Short. Eat Biscuits!
by Amy Jordan Smith
96 pages $9.95

Loving Through Bars
Children with Parents in Prison
by Cynthia Martone
208 pages $21.95

Marilyn Monroe Dyed Here
*More Locations of America's
Pop Culture Landmarks*
by Chris Epting
312 pages $16.95

Movie Star Homes
by Judy Artunian and
Mike Oldham
312 pages $16.95

Offbeat Museums
by Saul Rubin
240 pages $19.95

Quack!
*Tales of Medical Fraud from
the Museum of Questionable
Medical Devices*
by Bob McCoy
240 pages $19.95

**Redneck Haiku — Double-
Wide Edition**
by Mary K. Witte
256 pages $11.95

**School Sense: How to Help
Your Child Succeed in
Elementary School**
by Tiffani Chin, Ph.D.
408 pages $16.95

Tiki Road Trip
*A Guide to Tiki Culture in
North America*
by James Teitelbaum
288 pages $16.95

Order Form 1-800-784-9553

	Quantity	Amount
American Hydrant ($24.95)		
Atomic Wedgies, Wet Willies and Other Acts of Roguery ($11.95)		
The Bad Driver's Handbook ($12.95)		
The Book of Good Habits ($9.95)		
The Butt Hello . . . and Other Ways My Cats Drive Me Crazy ($9.95)		
Calculated Risk ($24.95)		
Can a Dead Man Strike Out? ($11.95)		
The Dog Ate My Resumé ($11.95)		
Elvis Presley Passed Here ($16.95)		
Exotic Travel Destinations for Families ($16.95)		
Free Stuff & Good Deals for Folks over 50, 2nd Ed. ($12.95)		
French for Le Snob ($16.95)		
How to Find Your Family Roots . . . ($14.95)		
How to Win Lotteries, Sweepstakes, and Contests . . . ($14.95)		
James Dean Died Here: America's Pop Culture Landmarks ($16.95)		
The Largest U.S. Cities Named after a Food ($16.95)		
Letter Writing Made Easy! ($12.95)		
Letter Writing Made Easy! Volume 2 ($12.95)		
Life is Short. Eat Biscuits! ($9.95)		
Loving Through Bars ($21.95)		
Marilyn Monroe Dyed Here ($16.95)		
Movie Star Homes ($16.95)		
Offbeat Museums ($19.95)		
Quack! Tales of Medical Fraud ($19.95)		
Redneck Haiku — Double-Wide Edition ($11.95)		
School Sense ($16.95)		
Tiki Road Trip ($16.95)		

Shipping & Handling:		Subtotal _____
1 book $3.00	CA residents add 8.25% sales tax _____
Each additional book is $ .50	Shipping and Handling (see left) _____
		TOTAL _____

Name _____

Address _____

City _____ State _____ Zip _____

☐ Visa ☐ MasterCard Card No.: _____

Exp. Date _____ Signature _____

☐ Enclosed is my check or money order payable to:

Santa Monica Press LLC
P.O. Box 1076
Santa Monica, CA 90406
www.santamonicapress.com   1-800-784-9553